GUIDELINES

Ministries with Young People

Young People Connecting with One Another, the Church, and God

Cindy Klick
General Board of Discipleship

MINISTRIES WITH YOUNG PEOPLE

Copyright © 2012 by Cokesbury

This book is printed on acid-free paper.

ISBN 978-1-426-73666-7

All Scripture quotations unless noted otherwise are from the New Revised Standard Version of the Bible, copyright 1989, Division of Christian Education of the National Council of the Churches of Christ in the United States of America. Used by permission. All rights reserved.

Scripture quotations marked RSV are taken from the Revised Standard Version of the Bible, copyright 1952 [2nd edition, 1971] by the Division of Christian Education of the National Council of the Churches of Christ in the United States of America. Used by permission. All rights reserved.

Some paragraph numbers for and language in the Book of Discipline *may have changed in the 2012 revision, which was published after these Guidelines were printed. We regret any inconvenience.*

MANUFACTURED IN THE UNITED STATES OF AMERICA

Contents

Called to a Ministry of Faithfulness and Vitality

Y ou are so important to the life of the Christian church! You have consented to join with other people of faith who, through the millennia, have sustained the church by extending God's love to others. You have been called and have committed your unique passions, gifts, and abilities to a position of leadership. This Guideline will help you understand the basic elements of that ministry within your own church and within The United Methodist Church.

Leadership in Vital Ministry

Each person is called to ministry by virtue of his or her baptism, and that ministry takes place in all aspects of daily life, both in and outside of the church. Your leadership role requires that you will be a faithful participant in the **mission of the church**, which is to partner with God to **make disciples of Jesus Christ for the transformation of the world**. You will not only engage in your area of ministry, but will also work to empower others to be in ministry as well. The vitality of your church, and the Church as a whole, depends upon the faith, abilities, and actions of all who work together for the glory of God.

Clearly then, as a pastoral leader or leader among the laity, your ministry is not just a "job," but a spiritual endeavor. You are a spiritual leader now, and others will look to you for spiritual leadership. What does this mean?

All persons who follow Jesus are called to grow spiritually through the practice of various Christian habits (or "means of grace") such as prayer, Bible study, private and corporate worship, acts of service, Christian conferencing, and so on. Jesus taught his disciples practices of spiritual growth and leadership that you will model as you guide others. As members of the congregation grow through the means of grace, they will assume their own role in ministry and help others in the same way. This is the cycle of disciple making.

The Church's Vision

While there is one mission—to make disciples of Jesus Christ—the portrait of a successful mission will differ from one congregation to the next. One of your roles is to listen deeply for the guidance and call of God in your own context. In your church, neighborhood, or greater community, what are the greatest needs? How is God calling your congregation to be in a ministry of service and witness where they are? What does vital ministry look like in the life of your congregation and its neighbors? What are the characteristics, traits, and actions that identify a person as a faithful disciple in your context?

This portrait, or vision, is formed when you and the other leaders discern together how your gifts from God come together to fulfill the will of God.

Assessing Your Efforts

We are generally good at deciding what to do, but we sometimes skip the more important first question of what we want to accomplish. Knowing your task (the mission of disciple making) and knowing what results you want (the vision of your church) are the first two steps in a vital ministry. The third step is in knowing how you will assess or measure the results of what you do and who you are (and become) because of what you do. Those measures relate directly to mission and vision, and they are more than just numbers.

One of your leadership tasks will be to take a hard look, with your team, at all the things your ministry area does or plans to do. No doubt they are good and worthy activities; the question is, *"Do these activities and experiences lead people into a mature relationship with God and a life of deeper discipleship?"* That is the business of the church, and the church needs to do what only the church can do. You may need to eliminate or alter some of what you do if it does not measure up to the standard of faithful disciple making. It will be up to your ministry team to establish the specific standards against which you compare all that you do and hope to do. (This Guideline includes further help in establishing goals, strategies, and measures for this area of ministry.)

The Mission of The United Methodist Church

Each local church is unique, yet it is a part of a *connection,* a living organism of the body of Christ. Being a connectional Church means in part that all United Methodist churches are interrelated through the structure and organization of districts, conferences, and jurisdictions in the larger "family" of the denomination. *The Book of Discipline of The United Methodist Church* describes, among other things, the ministry of all United Methodist Christians, the essence of servant ministry and leadership, how to organize and accomplish that ministry, and how our connectional structure works (see especially ¶¶126–138).

Our Church extends way beyond your doorstep; it is a global Church with both local and international presence. You are not alone. The resources of the entire denomination are intended to assist you in ministry. With this help and the partnership of God and one another, the mission continues. You are an integral part of God's church and God's plan!

(For help in addition to this Guideline and the *Book of Discipline*, see "Resources" at the end of your Guideline, www.umc.org, and the other websites listed on the inside back cover.)

Called to Ministry with Young People

You have been called to ministry with young people—those journeying through adolescence and those emerging from their teenage years to find themselves navigating the unpredictable and full-of-firsts years of their twenties and thirties. This sacred and exciting leadership role comes with dozens of challenges to be addressed, countless opportunities to touch lives, and a myriad of blessings that you might never anticipate. Get ready for the journey of a lifetime!

Your ministry may be well-established or newly formed, flourishing or struggling, transforming lives or currently just marking time. Wherever you find yourself, you are in a position to work with others to offer vital and life-changing ministry. Your work may begin with young people already in your church's doors and will certainly expand beyond those walls to their friends, the community, and an unlimited realm of possibility.

Your own experience, or perhaps the experience you wish had been yours, of growing up in a church has likely influenced your call to be involved in this ministry. Perhaps you were nourished in a church home and mentored by adults who helped shape you, which stirs you to feel the importance of providing a similar environment to today's young people. Or, if you count yourself among many whose early religious experiences were infrequent, unpleasant, or nonexistent, you feel called to facilitate a journey for others that is different from your own.

Your position as a leader with young people is the basis for building relationships and leading by example. The most vital way people of any age experience the love of Christ is through their relationships with others. A primary focus of your role should be creating opportunities to build solid relationships—between youth or young adults and their leaders, among each other, and with Christ.

This Guideline covers an introduction to the ministry of a youth or young adult coordinator. Your church may describe this volunteer position differently and each church will require duties according to the number of young people in the congregation, the size of the church, or other unique factors.

If you are a staff person, new to a professional youth or young adult ministry, you will find this Guideline helpful as well. As you look at the many possible duties and opportunities, you will work with your volunteers to share these responsibilities and to support one another.

A Biblical/Theological Foundation

the church's mission, as the institution representing the collective people of God, is to make disciples of Jesus Christ for the transformation of the world. Each individual who is reached through this mission joins others to continue this transformational work. As United Methodist Christians, our theological roots are planted firmly in the Bible and the work of John Wesley as the founder of Methodism.

The United Methodist Church was born from the teachings of Wesley, including the Wesleyan Quadrilateral. The Quadrilateral, based on the tools Wesley used for theological consideration, was so-named by theologian Albert Outler in the 1960s as four key components for study and decision-making in our daily lives. The Quadrilateral includes reason, experience, and tradition as important considerations, but Wesley upheld Scripture as the primary source of wisdom and inspiration. For those in positions of leadership in young peoples' ministries, Scripture should be the foundation on which relationships, activities, and faith communities are built.

The need for vital ministry with those who are young is evident throughout Scripture. The need for mentorship of those who are less mature, as they make their way as leaders in their own right, is illustrated by Old Testament teams such as Moses and Joshua or Eli and Samuel. In the New Testament, Paul and Timothy's relationship is a model for ministry. "These are the things you must insist on and teach. Let no one despise your youth but set the believers an example in speech and conduct, in love, in faith, in purity" (1 Timothy 4:11-12).

Every aspect of ministry with youth and young adults should be based in Scripture. Regular, intentional exposure to the Bible will help provide a developing knowledge of God's people, a new perspective on the past, and a compass for the future. Those who are leading, and training young believers to become leaders, will continue to learn themselves.

Relationships built on common study of God's word, covenant discipleship, and Christian friendship are the ultimate result of intentional ministry with youth and young adults. It allows those in relationship with each other to ask as John Wesley did in some fashion, "How is it with your soul?"

"Young People's Ministry"

Your role and the age range of people you will be serving should be defined by your church and its leadership, with guidance from *The Book of Discipline of The United Methodist Church*. If you have paid youth/young adult staff, the church's staff-parish relations committee will also be involved. The church's dedication to ministry with young people is outlined in the *Discipline* (see ¶256.3).

"The term *young people* is inclusive of all persons from approximately twelve through thirty years of age. The term encompasses both youth and young adult ministries and allows for age flexibility . . . in various cultures around the world."

"The term *youth ministry* is an inclusive title, encompassing all the concerns of the Church and all activities by, with, and for youth . . . [and] shall include all persons from approximately twelve through eighteen years of age . . . who are currently or potentially associated with the church or any of its activities."

"The term *young adult ministry* is an inclusive title, encompassing all the concerns of the Church and all activities by, with, and for young adults . . . [and] shall include all persons from approximately eighteen through thirty who are currently or potentially associated with the church or any of its activities."

Youth ministry may also involve students in 6th grade or even younger, depending on the middle school configuration in your local school system or your church's Christian education structure. Young adult ministry encompasses an even broader spectrum—from post-high school through college-age and beyond, single or married, with or without children.

Your ministry ideally will include families. In youth ministry, you will need to communicate effectively with parents and guardians and help your youth navigate relationship issues with parents, siblings, and other family members. Consider parents your partners in ministry, even if they are not "official" leaders. Their support will make a difference in their youth's spiritual journey. Consider ways to meet family needs, such as parent classes, support groups and seminars, and connect with your church's children's ministry to provide care for younger siblings during events and to plan transitional activities.

In young adult ministry, your umbrella of care may extend to the spouses of those in your group who are married; children of those who are parents; and perhaps the parents of young adults recently off to college, the service, or the world of work. Get to know the people who love the young adults you are called to serve.

First Things First: Establishing Priorities

Your ministry with young people should include as a foundation the same components as the membership promises that United Methodists make when they join the church: prayers, presence, gifts, service, and witness. Who you are, how you relate, what you do, and how youth and young adults experience you as a person and as a leader make all the difference.

PRAYER

You will need, desire, and benefit from God's guidance in your life and in your new role. Pray for an open heart and mind; opportunities to learn and to love; and specifically for the youth or young adults, their families and their issues, your church, your community, and beyond. You will be seen as a spiritual leader within your ministry and your congregation.

PRESENCE

Be there. For your ministry to be effective, young people must know that they can count on those called to be in ministry with them. Be prompt, dependable, and present. Spend at least as much time listening as you do talking, and make sure you offer your complete attention. Avoid allowing electronics and other distractions to take priority over the person and the conversation in front of you.

GIFTS

Be an example. It's hard to model generosity for others if you aren't on a journey that includes sharing your gifts with your church. Talk about the biblical concept of the tithe and give young people opportunities to give to a worship offering, to those in need, and to other worthwhile causes.

SERVICE

Serving others is one of the key ways people born in the last three decades are attracted to today's church. Offer short- and long-term, local and traveling mission trips, ways to serve that require some kind of sacrifice from you and your participants. Be open to new possibilities and to experiences and activities about which your group members are passionate.

WITNESS

You have become a role model in your new position. As a spiritual leader, the way you live, as much or more than the words you speak, becomes an example of your Christian integrity to those you serve. Be authentic and be the same person in every setting with your young people.

Getting Started—Youth Ministry

Youth ministry in The United Methodist Church provides a framework for youth to grow spiritually and relationally while they are developing physically, mentally, and socially. Strong, developmentally appropriate ministry activities and experiences provided by trained, caring adults is essential for a vital youth ministry. The *Book of Discipline* stresses its importance.

"There shall be a comprehensive approach to development and implementation of youth ministry programming at all levels of the Church. The comprehensive approach is based on the understanding of the primary task of youth ministry: to love youth where they are, to encourage them in developing their relationship to God, to provide them with opportunities for nurture and growth, and to challenge them to respond to God's call to serve in their communities. Four parts undergird this comprehensive ministry" (see ¶1119.2).

The *Discipline* goes on to describe those four parts, which include the production of curriculum resources, other resources for youth in the local church and at all levels of The United Methodist Church, leadership development, and general church structures that promote and support youth ministry.

Youth ministry should be broad-based and encompass a wide range of activities. In establishing your youth ministry, consider the resources of your church and the community, current and local trends in youth recreation and music, and input from your advisory and leadership teams. Always include youth in decision-making and planning for their ministry.

Learning with Partners and Teams

You probably will not step into a ministry vacuum, so you will want to start by gathering as much information as possible of the history, expectations, and plans (past, present, and future) of your church's youth ministry. Schedule time each week to talk with and get to know current and former adult volunteers with youth, parents of youth, the youth themselves, and pastor/church staff. Ask questions and seek answers, but even more importantly listen to the experiences, successes, failures, hopes, and dreams of those involved with past activities. Find out what has been happening, what is missing, what is working, and what is not. Your conversations will help you learn about the schools your youth attend; the activities that interest them; and their areas of temptation, struggle, joy, and triumph.

In addition to the history, there are key partners and potential helpers to consider. Do not limit yourself to only the adults and youth who have experience in your youth ministry. Seek out people who align themselves with your church but are not currently actively involved.

SOURCES OF CRITICAL INFORMATION

Not everyone with whom you speak will be a ministry partner. As you seek the insights of others into your youth ministry, obtained through conversations with parents; adults working with youth; pastors, staff, and lay leaders; the congregation as a whole; and, of course, youth, you will identify potential partners in ministry. Together, they are sources of critical information.

- **Relationships with youth.** As you get to know the teens who are involved in your church, your willingness to listen can facilitate a level of trust that will make deeper conversations possible. Visit with youth who are not presently participating in your youth ministry to cultivate that same level of trust, and you may identify what might engage them.

- **Conversations with youth workers in other churches or community organizations.** Share ideas, successes and challenges.

- **Resources within your church staff.** Talk with your clergy, Christian education, worship, and music staff members about their experiences with youth, ideas for resources, and ways you can collaborate in ministry. They can be important advocates and effective mentors for youth.

- **Resource persons within the United Methodist connectional system,** including district, conference, jurisdictional, and general church staffing. Young People's Ministries at the General Board of Discipleship can help facilitate these connections.

PARTNERS AND TEAMS

From your contacts, consider forming an advisory team of people who can help navigate the first year or two in your position. This group can provide extra ears and hands as you become established in your position. They can offer advice and guidance, help review resources, and screen volunteers. No matter the size of your church, a team-based youth ministry will better serve you and your youth.

Other possible partners or teams within the local church include a leadership team of youth and adults that sets the vision for youth ministry, plans activities and experiences, engages in outreach, makes fundraising and financial decisions, and evaluates effectiveness. As you seek adults and youth for these roles, think about building a gift-based ministry rather than filling slots with names. Help volunteers realize the blessing of melding their passions and their energy. This group may be the youth counsel, described on page 16.

A different team of adult leaders of youth might meet with you to discuss Christian education curriculum planning and implementation, practices of spiritual disciplines (Bible study, prayer, worship, etc.) within your youth ministry, and social aspects and current issues with youth (singly or together).

Another significant resource lies in the experience and expertise of youth workers at churches in your area, both within The United Methodist Church and from other denominations. A community ministerial association may be able to provide this list or you may need to seek out these contacts. Find and connect with these people in an effort to develop a network of support. The frequency of your need to meet with this group may diminish over time as your ministry becomes established, but make interfacing with colleagues a priority even after you feel comfortable in your role. These relationships will continue to provide support, insights, and new ideas for your ministry.

Coordinator of Youth Ministry

The process that led to your selection for this position, and your early conversations with others, should help you understand what is expected in your role. It is important for you to be flexible, to practice the art of listening, and to establish personal boundaries based on the amount of time dedicated to the position, whether you are a volunteer or paid staff.

RESPONSIBILITIES

Regardless of the size of the church and your program, youth ministry demands will vary by season and depth of engagement. You and your team(s)—a parent group, youth council, planning team—will be responsible for a variety of tasks and ministry options. Some are specified in the *Book of Discipline*; some will arise from your church and context. One of your greatest responsibilities is to make personal care a priority so that you are spiritually, physically, and emotionally equipped for ministry. The balance you create in your life will provide an example for those who are involved in your ministry.

Many of these responsibilities will be described more fully in this Guideline. In addition, you will find numerous specific suggestions for activities and experiences that carry out and support your ministry.

According to the *Book of Discipline* (¶256.3a), you will:

- Recommend to the church council activities, program emphases, and settings for youth.
- Use available resources and means to inform youth concerning the Youth Service Fund (see page 26) and cultivate its support.
- Challenge youth to assume their financial responsibilities in connection with the total program and budget of the local church.

Within your church context, you and your team will:

- Learn about and help your congregation to be aware of issues youth in your community might be facing.
- Help others find their gifts in youth ministry and train them to be effective in their roles as Sunday school teachers, youth group leaders, parents, mentors, etc.
- Help church leadership understand the primary task of youth ministry.
- Encourage inclusion of youth in congregational goals and decision-making. Help your youth be seen and heard beyond the walls of a designated youth space.
- Support, guide the work of, and convene regularly a council on youth ministry/youth leadership team.
- Help plan and carry out a varied and wide-ranging ministry with youth, including worship, study, fellowship, and service.
- Make use of leader and spiritual development resources for youth and participate in frequent and effective training experiences.
- Act as a liaison with organizations, people, and resources within the church, denomination, and the community that relate to youth and youth ministry.
- Organize parents and other congregants in youth ministry to support activities such as meals, transportation, and fundraising.
- Mentor youth and facilitate their development as they emerge to become leaders in their church, community, and world.
- Coordinate Sunday school and youth group curriculum, recruit and train teachers and leaders.
- Keep accurate records of youth participation.
- Manage the youth ministry budget; if this is not a separate fund or account, advocate to establish designated youth accounts within the larger church budget.
- Lead *Safe Sanctuaries*® efforts to insure the safety of all participants in ministry experiences.
- Serve on other appropriate church committees as needed and encourage the addition of a youth member on church council, local church leadership groups, at annual conference, or elsewhere.

Ministry Ideas and Strategies

As you "help plan and carry out a varied and wide-ranging ministry with youth, including worship, study, fellowship, and service" you face an almost limitless number of options of what to do. In general, these options might be described as building relationships, planting seeds of faith, nurturing faith development and putting it into action, tending to body and soul, and celebrating ages and stages. Consider these suggestions for each area in your planning.

BUILD RELATIONSHIPS
- Develop ministries specially tailored to youth needs.
- Hold cultural and regional festivals and events.
- Host outdoor adventures such as skiing, rafting, and camping.
- Offer gateway (open and welcoming) recreational activities that are casual and comfortable enough for youth to invite friends.
- Hold fairs designed to explore higher education or careers or help prepare job or college applications.
- Participate in sports leagues.
- Hold a lock-in (at the church) or lock-out (in the community).
- Host weekday breakfast or lunch groups at or near schools.
- Observe current trends that may draw new youth to events (plan theme-based events such as an argyle sweater contest, four-square or ultimate Frisbee tournaments, or cupcake buffet).

PLANT SEEDS OF FAITH
- Conduct worship in traditional, contemporary, and alternative styles.
- Conduct confirmation and Christian education classes to explore the concepts of God and other fundamentals of faith.
- Hold retreats focusing on God's creation.
- Go on mission trips.
- Seek involvement with adult mentors who speak and live their faith.
- Attend district and conference retreats.
- Participate in fine arts disciplines, such as vocal and bell choirs, orchestra, drama, dance, and other groups that may participate in worship experiences.

NURTURE FAITH DEVELOPMENT AND DISCIPLESHIP
- Train youth for leadership in worship and Christian education settings.
- Include Sunday school sessions about famous and little-known people of faith.
- Offer studies of the history and structure of The United Methodist Church, including the names and stories of our faith.

- Form sharing groups based upon everyday experiences.
- Encourage relationships between younger youth and older youth, and between youth and adults, in leadership roles and mentoring ministries.
- Provide specialized training for small groups in areas such as leadership development and peer mentoring.
- Cultivate an attitude of acceptance for youth at any stage in the faith-development journey.
- Hold discovery sessions about domestic and foreign mission possibilities for individuals, as well as mission-based and ministry careers.
- Offer spiritual-discipline retreats (silence, fasting, prayer, journaling).
- Urge youth to pursue leadership positions at the local, district, and conference levels and beyond, including large-event planning and design teams.

FEED THE BODY WHILE YOU FEED THE SOUL

- Ask parents for input on special food needs; offering healthy choices as well as the traditional pizza, and alternatives for those with food allergies or restricted diets.
- Offer a regular, continental-style, Sunday morning breakfast, as well as snacks at most events.
- Turn work into a party by combining a service project with a barbecue; deliver Meals on Wheels with an out-to-lunch event.
- Combine food and adventure through a progressive dinner, once-a-week visit to a different ice cream or frozen yogurt shop, or a scavenger hunt followed by a picnic.
- Use food as a way to connect with other groups in the church and beyond; make and serve a dinner for senior adults in your church; set up cooking lessons for youth with skilled volunteers; deliver sack lunches or a hot meal to the homeless at a shelter or in a park.
- Debrief such experiences, offer appropriate Scripture, open and close with prayer.

HONOR AGES AND STAGES

- Mark milestones in memorable ways, such as a special luncheon for confirmation and a reception for seniors graduating from high school.
- Attend family events to which you are invited, such as graduation parties and scouting ceremonies. Church leaders can become like extended family to youth and young adults.
- Determine when advancement to the next stage/grade/level will occur and stick with your plan. All parents think, and rightly so, that their youth are special, but making exceptions for some opens you up to criticism and/or having to make the same allowances for all. Be consistent with your decision-making.

- Plan transitional events such as a retreat for children entering youth ministry, a camping trip for rising and graduating seniors, a mentoring session for high schoolers to help new middle schoolers.

The Council on Youth Ministry

The function of a council on youth ministry is to see that the best possible ministry is offered by your church. The council is designed to oversee all ministries for this particular age group in your congregation and to advocate for youth participation in the total life of the church. This is an important and necessary team designed for the betterment of your church, regardless of its size.

Consider the following possibilities, based on the number of participants. You may regularly call together all youth and their leaders. If your church is small, you can function as a single unit to plan for, implement, and evaluate all aspects of your ministry. You may choose to determine leadership for the course of a year or rotate or share responsibilities. As your ministry grows, consider establishing a council of a predetermined size and establish procedures for nominating, appointing, or electing team members, and designating leadership within the team.

Membership on the council on youth ministry should include both youth and adults at a ratio of two or more youth for every adult. The *Discipline* requires that at least one-half of the membership be youth who might represent and be regularly involved in Sunday school; junior and senior high fellowship groups; confirmation; other entities, such as youth choir or special ministry programming, such as outreach. Adult members should include any paid staff and representatives of lay or volunteer leaders and parents of youth.

RESPONSIBILITIES OF THE COUNCIL

The *Book of Discipline* (¶256.3a) states that "the coordinator of youth ministries and the youth council, when organized, shall be responsible for recommending to the church council activities, program emphases, and settings for youth. The coordinator and council shall use available resources and means to inform youth concerning the Youth Service Fund and shall cultivate its support, provided that prior to this cultivation or as a part of it, the youth shall have been challenged to assume their financial responsibilities in connection with the total program and budget of the local church."

Additional responsibilities may include:
- Evaluation of youth ministry programming, considering growth, depth and vitality.

- Coordination and scheduling of all youth events.
- Publicity and dissemination of information for youth ministry activities.
- Representation on the church council.
- Implementation of special youth-led events projects for the congregation, such as worship experiences and fundraisers.
- Supervision of designated ongoing activities.
- Cooperation with the committee on lay leadership to designate youth representation for various church boards and committees.

CREATING THE COUNCIL ON YOUTH MINISTRY

Some people will be members of the council by virtue of their position on the staff or another nominated position that relates to the church council. The committee on nominations may assist you in selecting youth and other adult members for the youth council. As you plan and recruit, keep the functions of the youth council in mind so that you select people with the gifts and skills needed for the task.

- **Decide what type of structure will be most effective** in your setting.
- **Consider how you will handle** finances, communication, accountability, calendaring, and other issues.
- **Meet with leadership in the church** for other insights into your ministry goals and proposed structure.
- **Work with the Lay Leadership committee** to develop job descriptions for proposed positions.
- **Seek church council approval,** necessary as well as helpful in investing other leaders in your program.
- **Evaluate effectiveness regularly** as part of an annual planning retreat at the minimum.

Getting Started—Young Adult Ministry

a leader of young adult ministry faces an initial task of discovery. Who are the young adults in your congregation? Are they in college, post-college, employed, seeking work, married, single, divorced, parents, or childless? Do they work on Sundays, so that any time for church activities is not on a traditional schedule? The likely answer is some combination of the above. This fluid population will require your ministry to be flexible and responsive to the world of firsts this age group is facing: first job, first marriage, first child, first home. Young adult ministry can be an anchor in a sea of movement during life transitions.

The Importance of Young Adult Ministry

Ministry with young adults is a critical area that can too easily fall through the cracks in today's church. Those who have grown up in a youth ministry may leave for education and career possibilities or may become less interested in church involvement. Young adults may be single, married, divorced, partnered, working, studying, parenting, or some combination. Their stage in life doesn't fit in a prescribed set of criteria, making the establishment of effective ministry particularly challenging. "Young Adults" is one of the categories in *Comprehensive Adult Ministries (Book of Discipline*, ¶1119.3).

"*Comprehensive Adult Ministries*—the [General Board of Discipleship] will assist congregations and conferences in developing comprehensive ministries by, with, and for adults. In keeping with the primary task of the board, adult ministries may include but need not be limited to: education and ministries with young adults . . . and single adults (i.e. widowed, always single, separated, and divorced), and intergenerational programs involving adults. Such a plan would include biblical foundation and study, developmental stages and tasks of adults, faith development and spiritual formation, and leadership training in various models of adult educational ministries.

"Responsibilities may include such supportive tasks as: identifying the needs and concerns of adults (i.e. young adults . . . and single adults); assessing the status of ministries by, with, and for adults in The United Methodist Church; collecting and disseminating pertinent data on issues, models, and programs that inform the leaders in local congregations, districts, conferences, boards, and agencies to strengthen the quality of faith and life of adults."

Young adults are among the people mainline Protestant churches are having the most difficulty attracting and retaining. Ministry, mission, and worship opportunities that nurture, involve, and maintain a healthy young adult population need to be priorities of a vital church.

Partners and Sources of Critical Information

Just as in ministry with youth, you need not engage in young adult ministry in a void. Even if you are beginning a new ministry, you are not alone. As you begin, consider these sources of critical information and consult with others who have a stake in or experience with young adult ministry.

- **Seek out insights of others into your young adult ministry.** Your contacts should include the pastor, staff, and laity leaders in your congregation to help you locate and get to know the young adults. Are some currently involved in the music ministry, Bible studies, church sports teams, or in teaching children?

- **Develop relationships with young adults.** As you get to know your population, meet individuals and small groups for coffee or lunch. Find out what they are looking for in a church home, where their interests lie, and how they spend their free time. This will help you build a ministry that meets their needs and taps their gifts.

- **Converse with leaders of other young adult ministries.** Check out community resources such as recreation centers, libraries, and coffeehouses to see what is being offered and who is attending. You may uncover potential partnership situations for meeting space as well as leadership and ministry ideas.

- **Do generational research.** Today's young adults are members of the Millennial Generation, those born after 1980. They are generally savvy in their use of technology, comfortable with multi-tasking, and less religiously affiliated than even the two preceding generations of Gen X and Baby Boomers. According to research at the Pew Research Center, Millennials are more likely to be attracted to a faith by vital mission work than through worship experiences (*Millennials: A Portrait of Generation Next. Confident. Connected. Open to Change.* February 2010). Millennials entered young adulthood during the era of the Oklahoma City bombing, school shootings at Columbine and Virginia Tech, and the September 11 attacks. Some view faith as unnecessary in an uncertain world.

Coordinator of Young Adult Ministry

Your church may have established the goal of nurturing and growing an existing young adult program or you may be starting from scratch. Your job will be to determine the scope of your young adult population; to learn about their life situations, plans, and dreams; and to develop activities and create experiences that fits their ever-changing needs. Your own experiences with school, employment, and family will provide valuable insights as you become a guide and mentor to maturing young adults.

RESPONSIBILITIES

The *Book of Discipline* sets the upward age of young adults as 30, but your responsibilities may encompass a broader age range, depending on the membership of the congregation and the needs of your church and community. The *Discipline* focuses on the younger end of the age range in its recommended ministries, particularly in its attention to college-age young adults, by recommending ministries that relate them to on-campus ministries (see ¶256.3d). It further suggests connection with United Methodist Women (¶256.5) and Men (¶256.6) and other "program" ministries (¶256.1a-d).

These other ministry areas to which you may guide young adults or with whom you may partner include:
- **The church school,** including classes and small groups that meet during the week and/or away from the church.
- **Accountable discipleship groups,** either as participants or leaders, which focus on the personal faith journey that extends into acts of compassion, justice, worship, and devotion under the guidance of the Holy Spirit.
- **Mission and ministry groups,** both domestic and foreign.
- **Support groups,** such as care and prayer groups; divorce recovery; grief recovery; parenting groups; and support for people who are suffering from chronic illness, including persons with mental illnesses and their families.

The Council on Young Adult Ministry

A young adult ministry council could include the coordinator of the ministry; a pastor or staff member; lay or volunteer leaders; and young adult representatives for all of the demographics and ministry areas served by your young adult ministry, such as recreation, study, fellowship, singles, married, or parents.

From your contacts, develop a team or task force that can help you establish goals for your ministry. By including young adults from the wide variety of demographics listed above, you can determine an initial path for spiritual, social, and recreational goal setting for those in their 20s and 30s. Consider a broad level of offerings, from introductory, no-strings-attached "night on the town" dinner gatherings to theme-based Bible, book, or video studies based on a specific topic or area of interest. Additional leadership for events and groups can come from within your expanding list of young adult contacts.

DETERMINE THE NEED FOR A YOUNG ADULT MINISTRY COUNCIL

The *Book of Discipline* does not mandate a council on young adult ministry in the local church. The coordinator of this ministry should evaluate, along with staff members and lay leaders, the need for and configuration of such a council. Depending on the demographics and size of the population you are serving, young adult ministry could operate separately or as an arm of adult or family ministries. Consider the following possibilities as you evaluate your unique situation.

- **Evaluate** the scope of current and future plans and assessed needs. Which ministry area in your church structure is the best fit for young adult ministry?

- **Invite** interested leaders to be part of a committee to explore the possibilities.

- **Recruit** people in whom you have seen gifts in this area; allow them to sign up if they are passionate about this ministry.

- **Receive applications.** If interest level exceeds the number of participants needed, consider an application process for the young adult council.

- **Discern** with a group of young adults and other stakeholders the work to be done and pray for God's guidance in the process.

If you do not have a need at this time for something as formal as a council, it is still wise to have a ministry team of at least three or four others with whom you can plan, share dreams and ideas, prepare for leadership, and divide responsibilities.

Where Youth and Young Adult Ministry Happens

for most of the historic life of the Christian church, people have found their way into its doors through a worship service or experience. A large percentage of the Baby Boomer generation (born between 1946 and 1964) who attend church today likely began worshipping with their families when they were young. But for the younger Gen-X (born between 1965-1980) and the Millennials (born after 1980), who may not have grown up in church-attending families, introduction to a faith community today is more likely to come through an invitation from a friend or an opportunity to be in service to others.

Your Setting

When youth and young adults come through the doors of a church, the pastor/staff, volunteers, and congregation are given the opportunity to offer a first impression that will make visitors want to return. A warm welcome, a setting that feels comfortable and inviting, and a reason to make a second trip are critical and not as easy to achieve as one might think. Many who are skeptical of modern religion will not give the church a second chance to make a good first impression. Take a hard look at your setting. Do your church's atmosphere, architecture, worship styles, and culture beckon anyone under 40 to take a second glance?

WORSHIP

Although actively involving youth and young adults in worship (music, drama, liturgy, ushering), is a step in the right direction, this does not ensure that the service speaks to the needs of those age groups. It is important that youth and young adults are also involved in planning for worship and that their feedback is sought and valued. Including leadership from these age groups on a worship committee and an advisory team for pastoral sermon content will provide opportunities for both input and learning.

CHRISTIAN EDUCATION AND FORMATION

Sunday morning, or whenever your worship services are held, provides an obvious window to offer Christian education and formation classes in a schedule that fits with worship service times. This is an important opportunity to offer a spectrum of learning and discussion venues for youth and young adults at any point in their faith journey.

Put in place a plan for your Sunday school or church school hour or hours by considering your audience, available space, and coordination with worship times. Your youth or young adults may be engaged by Bible or religious history classes, a clergy-led faith development course, or membership classes for confirmation-age youth or young adults.

A broad range of curriculum from The United Methodist Publishing House (Cokesbury) offers Bible studies, Wesleyan theology, and a United Methodist world-view. Be creative and adapt resources to fit your needs. Christian education settings for youth and young adults can go beyond the traditional to various small-group settings, the use of video clips or movie series, book studies, or topical discussion-based classes.

SOCIAL AND RECREATIONAL

The fellowship component of a ministry should offer fun with a Christian atmosphere and message and be made up of events designed to help youth and young adults connect with each other in a casual setting. The traditional youth group for teens has a long-standing history of providing a time and place to share food, build relationships, ask questions, seek and worship God, and discover what it means to be the church. As youth traverse the path from junior high to high school and into young adulthood, they can be transformed to live lives of faith and cultivate Christian values within the arms of a caring, connected community.

A small-group setting for any age and stage has the best chance for success when it meets in a regularly-established pattern. Community is built quickly with more frequent meetings, perhaps weekly instead of monthly. Consistency of leadership, time, and space is more important than any particular day or timeframe. Leaders should be open to consider meeting times other than the traditional Sunday if another day is a better fit for the group.

An opportunity to check in with each other and share joys and concerns is vital. A group that listens to each other and prays together will develop a deeper connection. Consider the introduction of Scripture in each setting as well. These are the elements that make us different from other organizations in which our youth and young adults may be involved. Remember that we are not called to duplicate the calendar of the neighborhood recreation center, but to offer Christian fellowship, education, and formation.

Whether your group contains youth or young adults or both, many members of this generation become invested in their faith through action: service projects, short-term mission experiences, camping, and recreation. Consider planning for multiple learning styles in activities as well as worship experiences, including auditory, visual, and kinesthetic. Providing a variety of opportunities will speak to the needs of more participants.

STUDY IN GROUPS

Special study groups provide the small-group settings essential to church vitality. A small group of peers can set the stage for a deeper level of faith development, study of a particular interest area, or discussion of a relevant topic. A Bible study such as DISCIPLE: *Becoming Disciples through Bible Study* offers several levels, including a youth version, and is a nine-month weekly study that builds strong community, commitment, and Christian discipleship.

The possibilities are endless. High school students or young adults may be engaged by a class on faith development that explores the Social Principles and other doctrines of The United Methodist Church. Confirmation or other membership classes should be available for those who are interested and did not confirm their faith at a younger age. When establishing a group, consider the age range of those involved. Too small a group may not be viable, but members of a group with a very large age span may not share enough common ground to connect well with each other.

MISSION PROJECTS

Mission trips, whether local, around the country, or around the world, are invaluable tools for helping youth invest in their faith and put their beliefs into action. They also can be an important entry point into church life for youth and young adults who find a connection to God in service to others. If service is the entry point, it is important to add the biblical and faith foundation either during or after the experience so that the participants understand their service as ministry and not just an adventure. It is **crucial** that mission experiences in another culture (even within the United States) be grounded as well in an understanding of hospitality. Understanding and appreciating the culture of the people served in mission promotes rewarding relationships and avoids the danger of patronizing or marginalizing them.

National church and secular organizations such as Sierra Service Project, Appalachia Service Project, Habitat for Humanity, United Methodist Volunteers in Mission, and denominationally sponsored mission experiences can be starting points, especially if you need help finding a location to serve and are unsure how to make plans for a trip. Some agencies have age restrictions, such as age 16 and older for most Habitat locations, so be sure to ask questions and read guidelines carefully to ensure that your prescribed trip meets the needs and demographics of your youth or young adults. Your church can create its own mission experiences once you and other leaders feel comfortable doing so. The General Board of Discipleship (www.globalyoungpeople.com) and General Board of Global Ministries of

The United Methodist Church have developed websites that feature many mission opportunities as a resource for youth groups and young adults. Churches in other cities and countries can also be great resources.

Investing time and money in your own community is essential as well. Local food and clothing banks, senior adults, and veteran's agencies are among the organizations that will welcome your efforts.

ADDITIONAL INVOLVEMENT IN AND BEYOND THE CHURCH

Youth and young adults in your church may have needs and desires beyond the scope of your ministry offerings, and you can help them make rewarding connections. The pastor/staff of your church and other ministry centers, as well as those who work with youth and young adults in community settings, will have ideas and connections. Possibilities include:
- United Methodist Women, United Methodist Men
- Boards, councils, committees of the local church
- The larger Church: The United Methodist Church at the district, conference, jurisdictional, and denominational levels
- Interdenominational youth and young adult ministry opportunities, which may provide an opportunity for discussion of theological similarities and differences among denominations
- Community recreational offerings and organizations such as Boy Scouts and Girl Scouts
- Camping and Retreat ministries

CHRISTIAN PRACTICES AND DISCIPLINES

The mission of the church is, with God's help, to make disciples of Jesus Christ for the transformation of the world. It follows, then, that the ultimate goal of our ministries together is to help youth and young adults develop a deep, sustainable relationship with God, nurture the spiritual and human relationships in their lives, and mature in their faith and character. Spiritual disciplines have been encouraged as a regular and integral part of United Methodism since the days of founder John Wesley and include:
- Worship of God, as a believer and part of a community
- Reading the Bible to hear, study, and meditate on the Scriptures
- Prayer, individually and as a corporate body, an essential part of Christian living
- Fasting, per the examples of Jesus and the Bible
- Communion, as a tangible example of God's grace
- Works of mercy, or doing good on behalf of other people
- Tithing, moving toward donating at least ten percent of resources

YOUTH SERVICE FUND

The Youth Service Fund (YSF) is part of Young People's Ministries and gives youth the opportunity to give money and time to projects that they design, lead, and implement. Funding for YSF is collected and raised at the local church level, with 70 percent remaining in local communities through the annual conferences. The remainder is distributed by the Division on Ministries with Young People to fund youth-designed and youth-led projects around the world, selected by a project review committee, and for resource promotion and interpretation. An ongoing goal is to increase involvement in contributing to YSF to include annual conferences from around the world in addition to those from the United States.

Any youth organization may apply for funding, with applications due by June 1 each year for project selection for the next calendar year. Project categories, designed to serve those in need, include Faith Sharing and Outreach, Leadership Development, Scholarship, Ministry with At-Risk Youth, and Agricultural/Vocational.

Money raised by youth in local churches is sent to the treasurer of the annual conference. Seventy percent of the money is administered by the annual conference. The Conference Council on Youth Ministries or equivalent structure decides how grant requests will be funded. The remaining 30 percent is sent to be administered by the Division on Ministries with Young People.

Connectional System:
You Are Not Alone

Coordination of youth and young adult ministry at a higher level than the local church is prescribed in the *Book of Discipline*. Seek information and connections from the district, conference, jurisdictional, and general levels of The United Methodist Church to provide additional resources and opportunities for your ministry. Youth and young adults should be offered the opportunity to represent the local church at annual conference and to apply for the design and planning teams for regional, national, and international events. These annual conference and jurisdiction organizations and leaders may provide help for you:

- The annual conference council on youth ministry (*Discipline*, ¶649.1) or conference council on young-adult ministry (¶650.1)
- The district coordinators for young adult ministry (¶665)
- The district council on youth ministry (¶672)
- The jurisdictional young adult organization (¶534)
- The jurisdictional youth ministry organization guided by a coordinator, which hosts a convocation, at least every other year (¶533)

The Division on Ministries With Young People (DMYP), within the General Board of Discipleship of The United Methodist Church, serves youth and young adults at a denominational (or general church) level (¶1201). DMYP was created to connect young people and those in ministry with young people, to each other, to the church and to God. This division provides a central resource for ministry with young people and strives to "empower young people as world-changing disciples of Jesus Christ, to nurture faith development, and to equip leaders by:

- **developing youth/young adult spiritual leaders** of local congregations to transform lives by making disciples of Jesus Christ;
- **challenging** The United Methodist Church to embrace, confirm, and celebrate God's call on the lives of young people;
- **cultivating and nurturing** life-giving ministries where influence and worth are not limited by age or experience;
- **advocating** for the issues and concerns of young people in the church and the global community;
- **empowering** young people to work as agents of peace, justice, and mercy;
- **building a network** of support and providing resources that connect the diverse experiences of youth and young adults in local ministries and communities across the globe."

Vital Leadership for Your Ministry

W hether your ministry is with youth or young adults, choosing, developing and training leaders will be a top priority on your list of responsibilities.

Leaders model a Christian lifestyle, can offer advice and guidance without judgment, and genuinely enjoy the company of the youth and young adults. They need not fit any age profile (except as described in *Safe Sanctuaries* for reasons of safety and prudence). Variety in age, marital status, family structure, career, and background offers a broad spectrum of experiences to be shared and provides a more familial-type setting.

Good leaders possess recognizable qualities. Ask the youth or young adults in your ministry who they know that fits the leadership profile you develop together. Leaders can be parents of youth. Consider connecting parents of students as leaders in a parallel setting, similar programming with another age group, rather than with their own teen.

Well-Trained Leadership

Leaders who are open to new ideas and who listen to the thoughts of the young people they serve will continue to learn and grow. Consider these possibilities to provide insight for and guidance of your ministry's adult leaders:

Training events led by district and conference coordinators or staff of youth or young adult ministries. These persons may have a schedule of upcoming training events, be able to plan an event to meet your special needs, provide training at your church, or recommend other qualified professionals to do so.

The General Board of Discipleship offers on-site and online training opportunities. Contact your conference youth coordinator or Young People's Ministries at GBOD (see Resources).

Community opportunities for education and training may be offered by hospitals, mental health networks, law enforcement agencies, social service offices, and other governmental units. Such workshops and seminars often pertain to youth and young adult ministry and may be free or low-cost.

Collaboration with other churches may allow you to bring in professional speakers or other guests that you might not otherwise be able to afford.

An interdenominational network can help make you aware of community events about teen suicide, addiction, family conflict, or other pertinent topics.

When you are planning for the venue and leadership of your training events, keep these tips in mind.

- **Offer to potential leaders** (who have successfully completed a background check, if working with youth) **the opportunity for a trial run** of a few sessions or as a substitute in the ministry setting in which they will work. Partnering with a veteran leader will enhance the experience for the new volunteer, help them begin to know the youth or young adults, and become familiar with the format of the ministry.

- **Provide resource materials** for training and for ministry well in advance, allowing leaders to become comfortable with curriculum and lesson plans. Acquaint new leaders and teachers with different learning styles in your training methods.

- **Explain the planning process** for long- and short-term activities, experiences, and special events.

- **Define the structure of your ministry,** including a council or leadership team, and how volunteers relate to this structure.

- **Provide time for new leaders to ask questions** and to interact with each other.

- **Give leaders a support network** on which to rely as they become comfortable in their new roles.

Youth and Young Adult Leaders

For any of us to lead others, we must first have followed other effective leaders. We learn much of what we know, including leadership skills, from our experiences with other people. During junior high and high school participation in youth ministry, teens will grow spiritually, emotionally, and physically. They can learn what it's like to be a part of a Christian community and gradually take on the leadership skills needed to help create and sustain that community. These suggestions do not preclude youth or young adults being included in any of the training opportunities already mentioned.

YOUTH LEADERSHIP OPPORTUNITIES

In the spirit of "It takes a village to raise a child," the *Discipline* charges pastors, parents, guardians, sponsors, godparents, church leaders in Christian education and formation, scouting leaders, and other members to provide training for children that will lead to a personal commitment to Jesus Christ and will enable them to live out their baptismal vows (¶226.4). Obviously the whole congregation has responsibility in being models, mentors, and Christian brothers and sisters to the children of the church and neighborhood.

Youth, while minors and thus, legally children, still have a stake in the Christian upbringing of their peers and of younger children. They learn to lead by seeing good leadership from others. Consider these pointers in planning for developing youth as leaders.

- **Lead by example.** Youth have the ability to influence the way other youth think. Help develop young Christian leaders who are positive examples, rather than negative leaders, among their peers.

- **Lead through teamwork.** As a member of an elected council or part of another type of leadership team, youth have the opportunity to guide the direction of the youth ministry in their church. Older and younger youth can learn from each other and be accountable for their commitments to the rest of the team.

- **Lead with other leaders.** Because confirmed youth are full and equal members of their local church, The United Methodist Church requires youth representation on every church board or committee except trustees (trustees must be of legal age). This policy of representative youth, ages twelve to eighteen, applies from the local church through all general boards and agencies.

- **Lead in a gifts-based ministry.** The better you get to know the youth in your ministry, the better you are able to help them connect to leadership opportunities that explore and develop their gifts. Youth will be much more engaged as part of the body of Christ if they are learning to lead in an area in which they can identify and develop skills and passions.

YOUNG ADULT LEADERS

Young adults may come to your ministry with or without past church involvement and with a broad range of leadership experiences from within and outside of the church. They may be enthusiastic or reluctant, trusting or skeptical of your leadership and of their own abilities in this area. As you and they get to know each other, you can help each one explore a call to leadership and provide opportunities in many areas. The *Adult Ministries Guideline* contains information that may be helpful in this area.

MIDDLE AND OLDER ADULT LEADERSHIP

Youth and young adults need leaders who have walked in their shoes, who have experienced teenage angst, struggled with higher education decisions, and searched for that first job in their twenties. Because these are relationship-based ministries, consistent, effective leadership is essential in developing and maintaining strong programs. It is more important for adult leaders to be good listeners, committed to their constituents, flexible, and able to adapt to changing situations than it is for the leaders to be from the same generation as the youth or young adults. Safe Sanctuaries® practices require an age span of at least five years between adults and the youth they lead. Leaders of young adults will want to consider boundaries in their ministry as well.

CLASSROOM LEADERSHIP

Sunday school, confirmation, young adult classes, and other small groups for young people require commitment to regular presence, use of training and resource opportunities, and a willingness to explore and discuss the difficult questions of the Christian faith. Strive to recruit and establish teams of two unrelated adults for each setting.

For leaders to be enthusiastic about such an extensive commitment, they need to be invested in the importance of their role. The elementary school classroom process of looping, or keeping teachers or leaders with the same group of students for more than one year, can be very successful in large- and small-church settings. Leaders and students get to know each other, build strong relationships and are accountable to each other to continue together. Strong, effective leaders who receive regular training and help with developing resource materials can lead the same group of youth throughout junior high and high school or stay with young adults through their college years, career transitions, and changing family structures.

FELLOWSHIP, SOCIAL, AND RECREATIONAL LEADERSHIP

Ministry with youth and young adults can be a combined ministry of friendship and discipleship. Regular church youth group gatherings need consistent adult leaders who offer humor, compassion, fun, and guidance. People who spend a great deal of time together, in a youth group setting or young adult social network, recreational pursuit, or sports league will become close by virtue of shared experiences. Leaders can offer adult wisdom on choices made, perspective on consequences rendered and the grace and forgiveness that come from the love of Christ. Leaders can be a positive example that any particular age and stage can be enjoyed as well as survived and is a springboard for future growth and development.

Realistic Job Descriptions

Regardless of the age of your leaders or the age of those they lead, clear guidance regarding expectations is essential. A job description should include placing the position within the context of ministry throughout the church. It is especially helpful in larger churches with myriad volunteers and activities to have something in writing. At the very least, any teacher or other person working with your youth and young adults should have a clear conversation about expectations.

Consider these points.

- The leader's role should be clearly explained with time required for preparation, the time span of the commitment (beginning and ending), and defined expectations.
- Teams of leaders should be assigned based on compatibility, availability, and experience. Pairing a veteran with a newcomer may be the way to bring up less confident volunteers.
- Human and material resources should be readily available, training opportunities outlined, and completion of regular training expected and required.
- Peripheral, or related, expectations should be clearly outlined, such as attendance at committee meetings or other outside events.
- Financial or other potential ramifications, such as need to purchase supplies, should be made clear.
- While it might be assumed, you can also present the personal and spiritual characteristics you desire in any volunteer. If part of the role is helping others in faith formation, you want your leaders to be mature in their faith as well.

Pastor/Church Staff Support

Church staff can be valuable support for you and your ministry plans. Ask for their guidance and suggestions, and keep them informed of your plans and events. They can communicate the importance of young people's ministry to the congregation, be advocates on behalf of your ministry, support emerging youth and young adult leaders, and participate as available in various classes or events. Youth and young adults will likely respond well to the opportunity for a book group, movie discussion, or theological debate with the pastor or another leader.

Across the congregation, the pastor, staff, and other leaders may support and assist in your ministry to young people in other ways.

- Pastoral care by trained, experienced church staff can be very helpful in counseling youth and young adults and helping them develop their own skills as peer counselors.
- Worship leaders can encourage participation by youth and young adults as musicians, lay readers, ushers, sound technicians.
- Short-term studies with staff and lay Christian education leaders can offer youth and young adults new topics of exploration on their faith journey.
- Appointment to various committees can be encouraged for youth and young adults by the pastor as chairperson of the committee on lay leadership.

Tool Box for Leaders in Your Ministry

Leaders of young people should be consciously working to improve their skills as spiritual leaders. Just as John Wesley said that Christians are, with God's help, moving on toward Christian perfection, leaders are on a journey that is never complete. They should be questing continually for new information and better understanding. Training is particularly helpful in the following areas:

- Theology and philosophy of youth and young adult ministry
- Youth and young adult culture: music, technology, sexuality
- Introduction to curriculum resources: finding, adapting, and using
- Parent training and understanding of other family relationships
- Risk management and Safe Sanctuaries® procedures
- Church budget process
- Time management
- Event planning, short- and long-term
- Relational, organizational, and spiritual guidance skills

The following lists of assets equip a "toolbox" of leadership skills in youth and young adult ministry.

Relational Skills

Leaders in the church, whether they are youth, young adults, or more mature adults, will find themselves in many types of relationships within small groups, committees, and other types of ministry programming.

BE A PARTNER IN LEARNING

Leaders and those they are leading have a lot to learn from each other. Every participant's unique insights, perspectives and talents contribute to building connection within the group. Each person's efforts to accept and care for others will enhance the experience, helping members feel valued by and valuable to the group.

REQUIRE ACCEPTABLE BEHAVIOR

The behavior of leaders, youth, and young adults should be age-appropriate. The role of adult leadership should be that of mentor and teacher rather than pal and confidante. Establishing and maintaining boundaries is critical, as indicated in the Safe Sanctuaries® practices (see page 37).

GET TO KNOW EACH GROUP MEMBER

Leaders' efforts to get to know each person individually will encourage other group members to build relationships and develop camaraderie. Newcomers are more likely to return to a setting where they are made to feel important to the group during their first meeting.

COMMUNICATE

Leaders who regularly use a variety of communication tools will reach more participants from this technologically savvy generation. Consider texting; e-mails to parents of youth; postcards; calendars; church website and publications; and social media, such as Facebook. Promote what's happening, ask for ideas and input, use pictures and graphics to attract attention. Consider a separate Facebook page for your youth group or young adult class and take advantage of posting events through Facebook to get RSVPs for specific activities.

Remember that your status as a role model continues into social media. Be careful of what you write, photos that you post, groups you decide to join, and keep personal/professional boundaries intact. Never post a photo that includes minors if you do not have permission. In the Facebook friend request process, let youth or young adults make the first move.

BE A GOOD LISTENER

Practice listening so that the speaker feels he or she has your attention and that you are not distracted by other people, technology, or your surroundings. Youth or young adults are more likely to put their trust in a leader who listens well, is readily available, and responds appropriately to a plea for help.

Your constituents will know you have been listening when you are able to reply with a well-thought response. Sometimes they may be seeking only listening ears and need affirmation that they were heard rather than a specific answer. Even when you don't have immediate answers, you can offer thoughts on other helpful resources and look for solutions or help together. Remember that *listening* does not mean *fixing* or *counseling*.

BE APPROPRIATE AND CONSISTENT

Set reasonable standards and boundaries in areas such as clothing, language, behavior, public displays of attention, and media. Consider codes of conduct or behavior covenants for all events and especially for offsite trips and retreats, then hold young people accountable for following guidelines and adhering to established rules. Expect leaders to be examples of integrity as well and to follow established rules of accountability. Remember that mistakes will be made and leaders have the opportunity to be an example of God's grace and forgiveness.

SHARE YOUR STORY
Your youth and young adults will be interested in hearing about your experiences, your faith journey, and your call into this ministry. These conversations will be most effective as dialogue rather than a lecture.

BE AFFIRMING AND ENCOURAGING
You have the opportunity to be one of the important adult figures in the lives of young people in your ministry. By getting to know them as individuals and recognizing and affirming their gifts, you can help them develop confidence in their leadership skills, interests, and talents. Ask questions, show interest in each person, and recognize and acknowledge their special attributes.

Some youth or young adults may be hesitant to become involved in a specific class, program, or event. Leaders can encourage them to step outside their comfort zone; an invitation from a peer can also provide incentive. Be sensitive and caring while encouraging their participation. The transformation of a youth from junior high through high school or of a young adult from late teens to mid-twenties doesn't happen overnight, but is nonetheless miraculous to observe. You will be blessed to walk alongside the youth and young adults on this journey.

TRUST AND EMPOWER OTHERS
Leaders become trusted individuals in the lives of young people by being approachable, consistent, and reliable. Be available when you say you will be, try to behave as a person of integrity in every setting, and never betray a confidence. When you need to take potentially dangerous or hurtful information to a parent or other third party, explain why this is necessary, then make sure the youth or young adult understands your position and is in a safe place.

Your role allows you to help young people succeed in endeavors they might never have considered and to learn from their mistakes along the way. Leaders can help uncover latent abilities, develop decision-making skills, pick up the pieces to move forward when things don't go as planned, and celebrate successes along the way. Empowering other adults as leaders in your program is essential to a team approach and a key to preventing burnout.

PARTNER WITH PARENTS OF YOUTH

If you are working with youth, remember that parents are your allies, not the opposition. You will not agree on every issue, but parents can be an excellent source for program volunteers, financial and emotional support, and insights into their teens' lives and issues. Get to know parents as you get to know their youth, but make sure they understand that information youth share with you is confidential.

SEEK AND OFFER SPIRITUAL GUIDANCE

Leaders in your youth or young adult ministry need to be devoted to their personal spiritual growth in order to better guide those they are leading in the spiritual disciplines of worship, Bible study, and prayer. Encourage your team of leaders with helpful personal resources and reinforce the importance of commitment to worship and personal growth. Study and small-group experiences with adult peers will help shape more effective Christian leaders, who can then model these disciplines for young people.

Adults who serve as mentors for youth and young adults need their own mature examples of Christian discipleship in the congregation. These relationships will help leaders continue to grow as well. Make sure your team of adult leaders has opportunities to be in service to others and to attend leader training and educational events beyond the walls of your church.

Safety Issues

Every annual conference has established the requirement for all churches to have Safe Sanctuaries® policies in place for the protection of children, youth, and vulnerable adults. *Safe Sanctuaries: Reducing the Risk of Abuse in the Church for Children and Youth,* by Joy Melton, has been developed specifically to assist churches in safety issues related to physical, emotional, or sexual abuse and the protection of leaders who work with minors. (There is an edition for pastors, as well; see Resources.)

SAFE SANCTUARIES

This resource is very important for churches as a whole, and youth and children's ministries in particular, to protect youth and children from any type of abuse and adult leaders and volunteers from being placed in a situation where they could be accused of abuse that did not occur. Safeguard your ministry by instituting the following Safe Sanctuaries® guidelines to be followed during all activities and experiences. Work with your clergy staff and board of trustees if changes need to be made. (Sample forms and worksheets are included in the Appendix.) The provisions here are addressed to youth ministry, but common sense and prudence should prevail for every age group.

- Adults applying to work with youth must complete a volunteer information packet and a background check, which is submitted annually through the state bureau of investigation.

- Two unrelated adults must be present with any group of youth; never just one adult present and never one adult alone with a youth.

- Adults must be at least 18 years old and at least five years older than the oldest youth present.

- Youth and adults never sleep in the same bed and preferably not in the same room on overnight events.

- One-on-one sessions are held only in rooms with uncovered windows and open blinds, open doors, or in highly public places.

- All meeting-room doors contain windows.

- Require annual leader training about abuse and Safe Sanctuaries®; have leaders sign a form stating that they have been trained and understand the issues involved. Inform volunteers about local laws on mandatory reporting of abuse.

- Make physical safety a priority by providing adequate adult supervision of all activities, professional safety training for mission trips, and a well-stocked first aid kit available at all times.

- Draft a medical permission form to be used for all events; include contact information, medical history, medications, and allergies. Consider a different colored form for youth and adults; check with your church's legal counsel about the possibility of a notarized form being kept on file to prevent the paperwork of a new form for each event.

- Mandate motor vehicle background checks for any adult driving youth, require the use of one seat belt per person in any vehicle being driven for a church activity; advocate for well-maintained, safe church buses and vehicles.

- Consult the board of trustees or executive director of church administration to become familiar with your church's insurance, making sure it is adequate for the scope of youth and young adult activities.

SEEK ADDITIONAL HELP

Safe Sanctuary® policies cover issues of abuse prevention, but other situations arise related to the safety and well-being of youth and young adults. Be cautious when confronted with issues beyond the scope of your skill and experience. Many problems facing young people require professional help, and you are absolutely not expected to fix or offer professional-level counseling for anyone. Establish a network of recommended experts in the mental health field, including counselors who work with youth and young adults; clergy and other church staff; school counselors; and help centers for issues such as suicide, teen pregnancy, and family planning for young adults.

Organization and Planning

Effective ministry requires the organization and implementation of dozens of details for every group, class, event, and activity within your ministry area. Communicate regularly with others leading ministry in your church to work together and avoid conflicts on your calendars and with human and physical resources. Use of technology will be critical in the success of your ministry, from the need for an attractive, easy-to-navigate website to a strong working knowledge of social media. Use these tools to reach youth and young adults where they are and to expand ministry possibilities beyond the walls of your church and local community.

SEE THE BIG PICTURE

If your ministry does not already have mission and vision statements, make that a first order of business for your leadership or planning team. Then discern whether your goals and strategies meet these criteria. Don't be afraid to change, reduce, or eliminate what isn't working or doesn't meet your ministry goals. Remember that the church is called to offer something different from and beyond the offerings of the local recreation center, club, or coffeehouse. Consider how those differences will be visible and known in your well-rounded ministry. Search for ways to make Scripture and prayer part of every event, whether it is spiritual or recreational; educate youth, young adults, and their leaders in the practice of spiritual disciplines and offer regular opportunities for those practices.

Remember to include a variety of settings and options. Young people, particularly youth, may also be quite young in the faith, but you will want to engage the more mature Christian young people in your ministry as well. If the flow of ministry in general is to reach out and receive people, to help to create and nurture a relationship with God, to equip them for ministry, and to send them forth as Christians into the world, your activities and experiences must serve that flow. Introductory events that are not intimidating or threatening to youth or young adults for whom church is a new experience will be a crucial first step for them. Once young people are acclimated and participating, the "come" events must be followed with opportunities for personal and leadership development as well as service. As young people come and go, you will need to plan for all of these kinds of experiences to recur regularly.

Remember, the point of origin for youth and young adult ministry does not reside only with you and your team. Young people may engage first through another group, ministry area, or activity, such as the choir. (Refer again to the section, "Where Youth and Young Adult Ministry Happens.")

PLAN AHEAD AND BE READY TO MAKE CHANGES

Set a calendar for at least a year in advance, considering topics for on-line and on-site classes, service projects, mission trips, social events, and so on, reserving needed spaces, vehicles, and speakers. This process will become easier after you have been in your position for at least a year. Remain flexible as well. Today's under-thirty population tends to live in the moment and you will need to include ministry components that are fluid enough to maintain attention. Topics for on-line blogs, opportunities to process local and world events when they happen, making and maintaining social media contacts will happen in-the-moment and not result from a leadership team planning retreat.

ENGAGE PARTICIPANTS

One of your goals as a leader is to be able to launch a class, program, study, or event from which you may eventually be able to step back as participants become comfortable taking on leadership and facilitation roles. In study/reflection groups an engaging theme breeds consistency; focuses the thoughts of youth, young adults, and leaders; and makes it easier for someone who has been absent to feel like part of the group when they return.

When a group grows too large for a space or its size becomes cumbersome for participants to be heard or to develop and maintain relationships, consider subdividing so that more young people have the opportunity to lead and contribute. Take advantage of technology as a tool for learning and relating and as a way for those in the group to contribute their skills and gifts to your ministry. Not every group, class, or activity need be a face to face group, especially with media such as Skype. Youth and young adults at college, for example, may be linked electronically for prayer, support, studies, or games. You might have a partner relationship for mission or study with young people in another region or country in this way.

For face to face activities, take attendance as a way to evaluate and measure participation as well as to follow up with those who are absent. Communicate in the ways most used by your participants. Text messaging, social media contact, and event invitations have taken the place of telephone messages, traditional mail, and even e-mail. Personal contact can make the difference in whether a group member returns to or disappears from your ministry.

BE RESOURCEFUL

Work with volunteer leaders to adapt resources to fit your ministry setting and welcome their suggestions for supplemental materials. Engage a skilled webmaster to make your webpage easy to use, attractive, and regularly maintained. Use a large variety of content, considering various learning styles of youth and young adults, and consider including on-line blogs, chat groups, and Bible studies. Explore church-produced materials but look to the world around you as well. The generation you serve will respond to the use of other books, movies, music, and speakers. Broaden your classroom concept to include coffee shops and homes, restaurants and clubs, libraries, and other community cultural facilities, in addition to on-line and within your church.

COMMUNICATE EXPECTATIONS AND OPPORTUNITIES FOR PARTICIPANTS AND LEADERS

Plan for more than you might need for a designated time frame; offer individual supplemental and optional activities so that a participant can be engaged beyond the limits of a class or event. In today's world of instant communication, your youth, young adults, and leaders have countless demands on their time and attention. Communicate with them clearly, frequently, and with the media they use. Help leaders feel confident and competent in their work with youth or young adults by offering annual, extensive training to incorporate use of technology, Safe Sanctuaries®, church policies, curriculum development, and special age-related issues. Use more frequent (monthly or quarterly) team meetings for leaders of specific areas and for topical discussions.

Evaluating Your Efforts

One important way to measure your progress in ministry is to develop ways to evaluate the effectiveness of resource components, leaders, the number of people being served, and how Christian disciples are being developed. More information is available in through www .umvitalcongregations.com. See particularly the "Measures Evaluation Tool" in the "Setting Goals" tab.

An Evaluation Process

Keep attendance for each event, tracking the numbers over a year and for the same time periods from one year to the next. Numbers can determine trends and are one measure of the vitality of a ministry. Remember to go beyond and beneath the numbers for stories of Christian transformation.

Analyze ministry progress regularly, at youth or young adult leadership team meetings, by reviewing what is happening in each area ministry, making notes about what is working and what needs improvement.

Lead an annual leadership team retreat and planning session to implement changes to be made, develop activities and experiences to be added, and analyze overall effectiveness.

Survey youth, their parents, young adults and the congregation, casually or formally, to obtain feedback on your ministry, its methods, leaders and programs. Surveys can be conducted in-house or by an outside professional, written, or on-line. Simple survey instruments, such as Survey Monkey, allow surveys of up to 10 questions for free.

Display a suggestion box or board for young people. Encourage participants' feedback on what they want to see, do, add, or eliminate.

Consider type and scope of planning as well as the number of people involved. Evaluate the number of leaders engaged; the ease or difficulty of obtaining commitment from caring, consistent adults; and the number of outreach opportunities extending beyond the church walls into the community.

Going Beyond the Numbers

How do you measure whether your efforts are influencing your target ministry population? Do you have tools to determine how your young people are progressing toward becoming committed disciples of Christ?

Paid and volunteer staff should work with your youth or young adult leadership team to establish numeric and financial goals, specific time periods for evaluation, and a flow of ministry involvement through an introductory level to deeper spiritual commitment and to emerging leadership. Persistent follow-up can help your team determine why some may leave from your ministry while others are there growing and deepening their relationship with God.

Consider creating a grid or graph for your ministry that includes the following categories. The easiest assessments are quantitative; that is, you can count or calculate them.

FOR QUANTITATIVE EVALUATION
- A list of activities, starting with the gateway type that welcome people in the door (including those that are offered off-site or on-line) and concluding with those that require the greatest commitment level
- The purpose of each event, class, or activity and the minimum number required to make it work
- The amount of paid/volunteer staff time needed to plan and execute
- The need and cost, in time and resources, to provide leader training to improve the effectiveness
- An ultimate goal for each entry in terms of the percentage that moves to the next level of involvement
- The total overall cost and the cost per participant
- Timeline for evaluation, as soon as possible after completion, to keep important details fresh in mind

Set reasonable and attainable ratio- or percentage-based goals that make sense in your context. For example, a goal of 20 percent greater participation of your existing population of young adults may be a more reasonable goal than 20 new young people, if you are in an area of population decline. What percentage of the youth or young adults on your membership role are actively involved in some kind of ministry? Of those involved, what percentage are regular in worship, opportunities for personal growth and study, and in outreach ministries beyond the walls of your church? How many disappear in the first month or year after their initial involvement? Whenever possible, conduct back-door interviews to ask why someone has stopped attending and what would help him or her consider returning. You may obtain vital information that can help you do an even better job of serving those who remain.

A too-common example of wasted energy is the continuation (or "life support") of plans and activities that no longer get the results you desire, even though "we've always done it that way." Use your evaluation and measurement efforts to their best end by being bold enough to pull the plug on something that has completed its effective life cycle in order to create space for something new and more effective to be born in its place.

FOR QUALITATIVE EVALUATION

Be sure to include goals and measures for the qualitative things you want to evaluate, particularly the results regarding the transformation of your young people as people of faith. "How many?" is a good question, but "How are we being formed as disciples?" is the point of ministry. These measures may not fit the chart, but they are the kinds of standards or indicators that tell you if young people are being formed more deeply in the image of Christ.

- The character traits you want your young people to cultivate, exhibit, and deepen
- The effect of their Christian practices, which will probably be borne out by the stories they tell and/or the witness of the community
- The new practices (spiritual or behavioral) that they take on
- The changes in leadership; how you see that people are gaining confidence to accept responsibilities and take on new roles
- Shifts in worship attendance and/or giving
- Anecdotes and observed evidence that young people are more loving, generous, hospitable, and service-oriented

If these standards are not being achieved, the "program" efforts may not be the issue so much as the relationships you have. More people will grow in faith by being with and emulating the mature Christians with whom they relate. So the "what" of your ministry efforts may not need to change so much as the "who" and "why" of what you do.

OTHER MEASURES

Remember to evaluate and measure your communications efforts as well. By taking stock of the time, effort, and cost required by each item on your grid(s), you can determine a few things that will benefit most from the greatest investment in communication. Consider which methods will best reach your intended audience.

Periodic evaluation of paid and/or volunteer staff is critical. (The pastor-parish relations committee will have the primary responsibility for professional staff.) Make every effort to match a person's gifts and graces with their specific role and design a two-way evaluation process that gives both parties the opportunity for feedback and positive suggestions for change. If possible, discuss the evaluations face-to-face, honor the contributions of every participant, and attempt to make changes when the situation is not a good fit.

Resources

** Indicates our top picks

YOUTH MINISTRY

The Adolescent Journey, by Amy E. Jacober (Downers Grove: InterVarsity Press, 2011. ISBN 98-0-8308-3418-1).

***Almost Christian: What the Faith of Our Teenagers Is Telling the American Church*, by Kenda Creasy Dean (New York: Oxford University Press, 2010. ISBN 978-0-19531-484-7).

Connect: Real Relationships in a World of Isolation, by Jonathan R. McKee (Grand Rapids: Zondervan. 2009, 978-0-810-28777-3).

Contemplative Youth Ministry: Practicing the Presence of Jesus, by Mark Yaconelli (Grand Rapids: Zondervan, 2006. ISBN 978-0-310-26777-5).

Creating an Authentic Youth Ministry, by Edward Fashbaugh II (Nashville: Discipleship Resources, 2005. ISBN 978-0-88177-406-1).

Devo-Zine Lifestyle Magazine: For Teens, By Teens (Nashville: General Board of Discipleship. ISSN 1088-0054).

Guidelines for Leading Your Congregation; see especially *Adult Ministries*, as well as *Small Group Ministries* and *Family Ministries* (Nashville: Cokesbury, 2012).

Jesus-Centered Youth Ministry, by Rick Lawrence et al (Loveland: Group Publishing, 2007. ISBN 978-0-7644-3504-1).

The Leadership Lab: A Leadership Development Resource for Senior Highs, by Hank Hilliard (Nashville: Discipleship Resources, 2011. ISBN 978-0-88177-597-6).

Losers, Loners, and Rebels: The Spiritual Struggles of Boys, by Robert C. Dykstra, Allan Hugh Cole Jr. and Donald Capps (Louisville: Westminster/John Knox Press, 2007. ISBN 978-0-664-22961-0).

OMG: A Youth Ministry Handbook, by Kenda Creasy Dean (Abingdon Press, 2010. ISBN 978-1-4267-0008-8).

Revisiting Relational Youth Ministry, by Andrew Root (Downers Grove: InterVarsity Press, 2007. ISBN 978-0-8308-3488-4).

Safe Sanctuaries: Reducing the Risk of Abuse in the Church for Children and Youth, by Joy Thornburg Melton (Nashville: Discipleship Resources, 2008. ISBN 978-0-88177-543-3).

**Sustainable Youth Ministry: Why Most Youth Ministry Doesn't Last and What Your Church Can Do About It*, by Mark DeVries (Downers Grove: InterVarsity Press, 2008. ISBN 978-0-8308-3361-0).

Thriving Youth Ministry in a Smaller Churches: Secrets of Cultivating a Dynamic Youth Ministry, by Rock Chromey and Stephanie Caro (Loveland: Group Publishing, 2009. ISBN 978-0-7644-4051-9).

What Is the Role of Teens in Your Church, by Dr. Jawanza Kunjufu (Sauk Village: African American Images, 2011. ISBN 978-1-9341-5549-3).

Wisdom on . . . Friends, Dating, and Relationships, by Mark Matlock (Grand Rapids: Zondervan, 2008. ISBN 978-0-310-27927-3).

Your First Two Years in Youth Ministry, by Doug Fields (Grand Rapids: Zondervan, 2002. ISBN: 031024045X).

Youth Ministry, by Jason Gant (Nashville: Abingdon Press, 2008. ISBN 978-0-687-65039-2).

Youth Ministry Management Tools, by Diane Eliot, Ginny Olson, and Mike Work (Grand Rapids: Zondervan, 2001. ISBN-978- 0-310-23596-5).

**Youth Ministry 3.0: A Manifesto of Where We've Been, Where We Are & Where We Need to Go*, by Mark Oestreicher (Grand Rapids: Zondervan, 2009. ISBN 978-0-310-66866-4).

Youth Pastor: The Theology and Practice of Youth Ministry, by Houston Heflin (Nashville: Abingdon Press, 2009. ISBN 978-0-687-65054-5).

YOUNG ADULT MINISTRY

10 Things Your Minister Wants to Tell You (But Can't Because He Needs the Job), by Oliver Thomas (New York: St. Martin's Press, 2007. ISBN 978-0-312-36379-6).

After the Baby Boomers: How Twenty- and Thirty-Somethings Are Shaping the Future of American Religion, by Robert Wuthnow (Princeton: Princeton University Press, 2010. ISBN 978-0-691-14614-0).

**Change the World: Rediscovering the Message and Mission of Jesus*, by Michael Slaughter (Nashville: Abingdon Press, 2010. ISBN 978-1-42670-297-6; four-session DVD with leader guide, ISBN 978-1426710124).

God's Politics: Why the Right Gets It Wrong and the Left Doesn't Get It, by Jim Wallis (San Francisco: HarperCollins, 2006. ISBN 978-0-06-055828-8).

Guidelines for Leading Your Congregation (See above. Nashville: Cokesbury, 2012).

***If the Church Were Christian: Rediscovering the Values of Jesus*, by Philip Gulley (San Francisco: HarperCollins, 2011. ISBN 978-0-06-169877-4).

Lasting Impressions: From Visiting to Belonging, by Mark Waltz (Loveland: Group Publishing, 2009. ISBN 978-0-7644-3747-2).

Living the Questions: Essays Inspired by the Work and Life of Parker J. Palmer, by Sam M. Intrator (San Francisco: Jossey-Bass, 2005. ISBN 0-7879-6554-5).

Millennials: A Portrait of Generation Next, Confident. Connected. Open to Change, by Pew Research Center, Feb. 24, 2010. Search the article at http://pewsocialtrends.org.

The Orthodox Heretic and Other Impossible Tales, by Peter Rollins (Grand Rapids: Zondervan, 2012. ISBN 978-1-55725-920-2).

Pilgrimage of a Soul: Contemplative Spirituality for the Active Life, by Phileena Heurtz (Downers Grove: InterVarsity Press, 2010. ISBN 978-0-8308-3615-4).

The Reason for God: Belief in an Age of Skepticism, by Timothy Keller (New York: Riverhead, 2009. ISBN 978-1-5944-8349-3).

Souls In Transition: The Religious and Spiritual Lives of Emerging Adults, by Christian Smith (New York: Oxford University Press, 2009. ISBN 978-0-19-537179-6).

Speaking Christian: Why Christian Words Have Lost Their Meaning and Power and How They Can Be Restored, by Marcus Borg (San Francisco: HarperCollins, 2011. ISBN 978-0-061-97655-1).

They Like Jesus But Not the Church: Insights from Emerging Generations, by Dan Kimball (Grand Rapids: Zondervan, 2007. ISBN 978-0-310-24590-2).

Velvet Elvis: Repainting the Christian Faith, by Rob Bell (Grand Rapids: Zondervan, 2006. ISBN 978-0-310-27308-0).

THE UNITED METHODIST CHURCH
The Book of Discipline of The United Methodist Church, 2012 (Nashville: The United Methodist Publishing House, 2012. ISBN 978-0-687647-859).

Division of Ministry With Young People, GBOD Tel. 877-899-2780, ext. 7058. E-mail: youngpeople@gbod.org. (www.globalyoungpeople.org). Sign up for the DMYP networks at www.gbod.org/youngpeople/email.htm.

United Methodist Curriculum Resources: The United Methodist Publishing House (Forecast, Curric-U-Phone, www.ileadyouth.com, and Sunday School: It's for Life at www.sundayschool.cokesbury.com). See the inside back cover.

The YouthWorker Movement (www.youthworkermovement.org) connects U.S. United Methodist youth workers.

www.YAnetwork.org Young adult information and resources for ministry.

20/30: Bible Study for Young Adults. A series designed for adult learners in their 20s and 30s. Each volume connects everyday life themes to Scripture and group action. Available from Cokesbury 1-800-672-1789.

Office of Family and Marriage Ministries, MaryJane Pierce-Norton, director. Ext. 7170; e-mail mnorton@gbod.org.